THE COLLEGE KIDS

Taking You On A Journey About College

Llevandote en una aventura a la Universidad

Written by Joe Johnson
Illustrated by Dominick Bedasse

CHICOS UNIVERSITARIOS

Taking You On A Journey About College

Llevandote en una aventura a la Universidad

Escrito por Joe Johnson
Ilustrado por Dominick Bedasse

The College Kids
Copyright © 2014 by Joe Johnson

Printed in the United States of America

First Printing, 2014

ISBN 978-0-9906092-1-6

TABLE OF CONTENTS

TABLA DE CONTENIDOS

THE COLLEGE KIDS

CHICOS UNIVERSITARIOS

The college kids are a group of four friends from Kalamazoo, Michigan. They are looking to explore the different colleges and universities in their state and share information with other kids.

Los Muchachos de la Universidad es un grupo de cuatro amigos de Kalamazoo, Michigan. Ellos ayudan a otros muchachos a explorar lo que significa poder ir a la universidad y en situaciones de la vida cotidiana.

SHAY

EMJAY

Meet the College Kids

Emjay is one of the smartest kids in his school and he also sings and raps better than a lot of older kids.

Shay plays all kinds of sports and her favorite class is science because she likes to do experiments.

Conoce los Universitarios

Emjay *es uno de los muchachos más inteligente de su escuela y también canta y rapea mejor que la mayoría de otros muchachos mayores.*

Shay *juega todo tipo de deportes y su clase favorita es la ciencia porque le gusta hacer experimentos.*

4

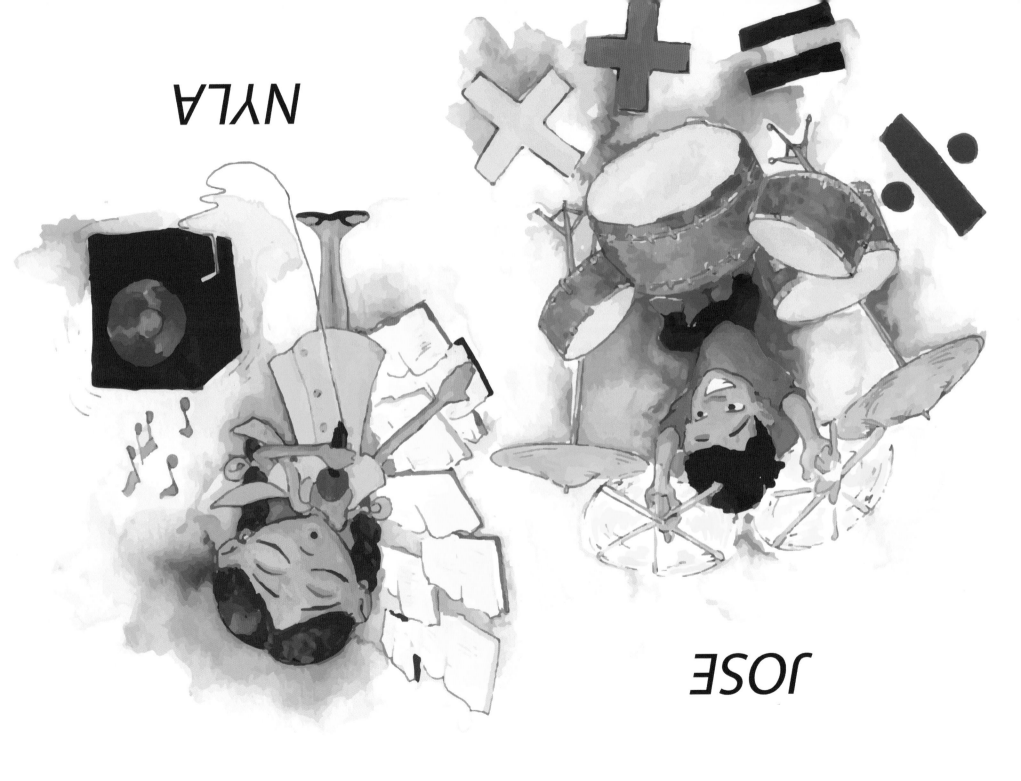

José loves to play the drums but he loves his math class because his teacher allows him to tutor his classmates.

Nyla is one of the best singers in the school but she loves reading books more than anything.

A **José** le gusta tocar la batería pero le encanta su clase de matemáticas porque su maestro(a) le permite ser tutor de sus compañeros de clase.

Nyla es una de las mejores cantantes en su escuela, pero más que nada, le encanta leer.

WHAT IS COLLEGE?

(Little brother and little sister drops off older brother at college.)

Little Brother: Wow! What is this place?

Little Sister: I don't know but it must be cool because our brother is moving here?

Little Brother: What is this place called?

Little Sister: Uh...I think...College

¿QUE ES LA UNIVERSIDAD?

(Hermanito y Hermanita dejan a su hermano mayor en la Universidad.)

Hermano menor: ¡Mira! ¿Qué es este lugar?

Hermana menor: No lo sé, pero debe de ser chévere porque nuestro hermano se va a mudar aquí.

Hermano menor: ¿Cómo se llama este lugar?

Hermana menor: ...Creo que se llama... la universidad.

(Little brother and little sister are
back in the neighborhood.)

Little Brother: I miss our brother...What is that
place called that he went to?

Little Sister: You forgot already? It's Called
COLLEGE!

Little Brother: Oh Yeah! Uh...What is college?

(Hermanito y hermanita
regresan a la vecindad.)

*Hermano menor: Extraño a nuestro hermano...
¿Cómo se llama el lugar a donde se fue?*

*Hermana menor: ¿Ya se te olvido? Se llama LA
UNIVERSIDAD.*

*Hermano menor: ¡Ah sí! ¿Qué es 'la
universidad'?*

Little Brother: Who are you?

Little Sister: Yeah...who are you?

Shay: My name is Shay!

José: My name is José!

Emjay: My name is Emjay!

Nyla: And my name is Nyla!

Shay: People call us the "College Kids."

Little Brother: Why?

Nyla: Because whenever young kids need to know about college, we come to save the day!

José: That's right...we want to teach you and your sister a little bit about colleges.

Emjay: It will be cool!

Little Brother: Ok!

Little Sister: Ok!

Hermano menor: ¿Quiénes son ustedes?

Hermana menor: Si... ¿quiénes son ustedes?

Shay: ¡Mi nombre es Shay!

José: ¡Mi nombre es José!

Emjay: ¡Mi nombre es Emjay!

Nyla: ¡Mi nombre es Nyla!

Shay: La gente nos llama "Los Muchachos de la Universidad."

Hermano menor: ¿Por qué?

Nyla: Porque cuando los jóvenes necesitan saber sobre la universidad, nosotros llegamos para salvar el día.

José: Sí, es cierto... Queremos enseñarles a ti y a tu hermana un poco sobre la universidad.

Emjay: ¡Va ser chévere!

Hermano menor: ¡Ok!

Hermana menor: ¡Ok!

College Kids: HERE WE GO!

Los Muchachos de la Universidad: *¡AQUÍ VA-MOS!*

COLLEGE INFORMATION

Emjay: There are many colleges around the world but we're going to visit some colleges in Michigan. But first... We have information for you!

1. To get into college, you must fill out an application from the college.

2. To pay for college, there are scholarships, grants, financial aid, and loans.

3. You are good enough for COLLEGE!

INFORMACIÒN DE LA UNIVERSIDAD

Emjay: *Hay muchas universidades en el mundo, pero vamos a visitar algunas universidades en Michigan. Pero primero... Tenemos informacion para ustedes.*

1. *Para poder entrar la universidad, tienes que llenar una aplicación de esa universidad.*

2. *Para pagar la universidad, hay becas, subvenciones financieras, ayuda financiera, y prestamos.*

3. *Tu eres lo suficientemente bueno para LA UNIVERSIDAD.*

WESTERN MICHIGAN UNIVERSITY

Nyla: Our first stop...Kalamazoo, Michigan. Western Michigan University (WMU)!

Shay: I love this place because my brother went here! I will tell you about this school.

José: That's fine with me!

Shay: Western Michigan University is in Kalamazoo, Michigan which is close to Lake Michigan. The mascot for WMU is "Buster" the Bronco. Students here live in dorms or apartments.

Little Brother: Dorms? What are dorms?

Shay: Dorms are where students live and they are just like bedrooms.

UNIVERSIDAD DE WESTERN MICHIGAN

Nyla: ¡Nuestra primera parada es... Kalamazoo, Michigan. La Universidad de Michigan Occidental!

Shay: ¡Me encanta este lugar porque mi hermano estudio aquí! Les contare sobre esta escuela.

José: ¡Esta bien conmigo!

Shay: La Universidad de Michigan Occidental se encuentra en Kalamazoo, Michigan y está cerca del lago Michigan. La mascota de la Universidad de Michigan Occidental es "Buster"; el bronco. Los estudiantes viven en dormitorios de la universidad o en apartamentos.

Hermano menor: ¿Dormitorios de la universidad? ¿Qué son dormitorios de la universidad?

Shay: Los dormitorios de la universidad son habitaciones en donde viven los estudiantes.

Nyla: That's right! Some dorms have bathrooms in them, one or two beds, desks, and other things for students.

Little Sister: Everybody lives in the same dorm?

Emjay: No. There are dorms all over campus and some people live in apartments.

José: Kalamazoo is pretty cool because they have something called, "The Kalamazoo Promise."

Little Sister: What is that?

Shay: The Kalamazoo Promise is a tuition scholarship for all high school graduates of Kalamazoo Public Schools. It's awesome!

José: Well, it's time to go to the next college!

Nyla: *¡Así es! Algunos dormitorios tienen baño, una o dos camas, escritorios, y otras cosas para los estudiantes.*

Hermana menor: *¿Todos los estudiantes viven en el mismo dormitorio?*

Emjay: *No. Hay dormitorios por todo el campus universitario y algunos estudiantes viven en apartamentos.*

José: *Kalamazoo es chévere porque tienen algo que se llama, "La Promesa de Kalamazoo."*

Hermana menor: *¿Qué es eso?*

Shay: *La Promesa de Kalamazoo es una beca de matrícula para todos los estudiantes de escuela secundaria que se han graduado de una escuela pública de Kalamazoo. ¡Es increíble!*

José: *¡Bien, es tiempo de ir a la siguiente universidad!*

Where do college students live?

¿Donde viven los estudiantes universitarios?

UNIVERSITY OF MICHIGAN

Little Sister: Wow! What is this place?

Shay: This is the University of Michigan or U of M and you are standing in the football stadium.

José: Also known as the "Big House.'

Little Brother: This place is big!

Nyla: It's big and it's the oldest university in the state of Michigan.

Little Sister: How can I come to U of M?

Emjay: There are lots of ways to get to college but the best way is to study to get good grades.

UNIVERSIDAD DE MICHIGAN

Hermana menor: ¡Wow! ¿Qué es este lugar?

Shay: Esta es la Universidad de Michigan o La U de la M y están parados en el estadio de fútbol americano.

José: También es conocido como "La Casa Grande."

Hermano menor: ¡Este lugar es grande!

Nyla: Es grande y es la universidad más antigua de Michigan.

Hermana menor: ¿Cómo puedo ser aceptada a La U de la M?

Emjay: Hay muchas formas de ser aceptado(a) a la universidad, pero la mejor manera es estudiar para obtener buenas calificaciones.

Shay: You also have to take the SAT or ACT.

José: Don't forget to fill out the college application and apply for financial aid.

Nyla: One more thing...try to find scholarships and grants to help pay for college!

Little Brother: Cool!

Emjay: Well, it's time to go!

Shay: *También tienen que tomar el SAT o ACT.*

José: *No olviden que tienen que llenar la aplicación de la universidad y solicitar ayuda financiera.*

Nyla: *Otra cosa más... Traten de encontrar becas y subvenciones financieras para qué les ayude a pagar la universidad.*

Hermano menor: *Chévere!*

Emjay: *¡Bueno, es hora de irnos!*

What do you need to do when preparing for college?

¿Que necesitas hacer en preparación para la universidad?

WAYNE STATE UNIVERSITY

Nyla: Detroit is so cool!

Little Brother: What do you mean?

Nyla: Detroit is the biggest city in Michigan and the Wayne State University campus is right downtown.

Emjay: Wayne State is also one of the largest universities in Michigan.

Shay: The campus is also close to where the Detroit professional football, hockey and baseball teams play.

Little Sister: Wow! That's cool!

José: More than half of the people that went to Wayne State University live in Michigan.

UNIVERSIDAD WAYNE STATE

Nyla: ¡Detroit es chévere!

Hermano menor: ¿Por qué dices eso?

Nyla: Detroit es la ciudad más grande de Michigan y el campus de la Universidad Estatal Wayne está en el centro de la ciudad.

Emjay: La Universidad Estatal Wayne también es una de las universidades mas grande de Michigan.

Shay: La universidad también está cerca de donde juegan los equipos profesionales de fútbol americano, hockey y béisbol de Detroit.

Hermana menor: ¡Wow! ¡Qué chévere!

José: Más de la mitad de las personas que fueron a la Universidad Estatal de Wayne viven Michigan.

Shay: But do not forget that you must go to class and graduate if you want to be added to the list of former Wayne State University students.

Emjay: That is true Shay! Showing up at school and going to class is important because if you are not at school in class, you cannot learn.

José: If you do not learn, you cannot go to college!

Nyla: I agree but it's time to go again!

Shay: *Pero no olviden que deben de ir a clase y graduarse si desean agregar su nombre a la lista de antiguos alumnos de la Universidad Estatal de Wayne.*

Emjay: *¡Eso es cierto Shay! Asistir a la escuela e ir a clase es importante porque si no vas a la escuela y a clase, no vas a aprender.*

José: *Si no aprendes, no puedes ir a la universidad.*

Nyla: *Yo estoy de acuerdo. ¡Pero es tiempo de irnos otra vez!*

What should students do to graduate from college?

¿Que deben hacer los estudiantes para graduarse de la universidad?

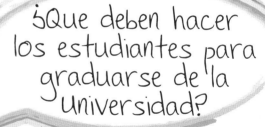

MICHIGAN TECHNOLOGICAL UNIVERSITY

Little Brother: Another university! Wow!

Emjay: This is Michigan Technological University!

Shay: Also known as Michigan Tech or MTU.

Little Sister: Why is there so much snow here!

José: There is a lot of snow in the winter and it's in the Upper Peninsula of Michigan.

Little Brother: Is there something special about Michigan Tech?

Nyla: The school is well known for engineering!

UNIVERSIDAD TECNOLÒGICO DE MICHIGAN

Hermano menor: ¡Otra universidad! ¡Wow!

Emjay: ¡Esta es la Universidad Tecnológica de Michigan!

Shay: También conocida como Michigan Tec o UTM.

Hermana menor: ¿Por qué hay tanta nieve?

José: Hay mucha nieve en el invierno y está en la Península Superior de Michigan.

Hermano menor: ¿Hay algo especial acerca de Michigan Tech?

Nyla: La escuela es conocida por ingeniería.

Emjay: That is true and they are also known for a game played by the student's called "Broomball!"

Shay: I heard it's a fun game and I also heard many of the students at this school studied hard in math and science classes before they made it to Michigan Tech.

José: That is true! You should study hard in math and science classes if you want to go to a school like this.

Little Sister: I am going to study hard when I go back to school.

Nyla: Good thinking! Well, it's time to go again!

Emjay: *Eso es cierto. ¡También son conocidos por jugar un juego llamado "Broomball!"*

Shay: *He escuchado que es un juego divertido, y también he escuchado que los estudiantes de esta escuela estudiaron muy duro en las clases de matemáticas y ciencia antes de atender Michigan Tec.*

José: *¡Es cierto! Deben de estudiar mucho en las clases de matemáticas y ciencias si quieren ir a una escuela como esta.*

Hermana menor: *Voy a estudiar duro cuando regrese a la escuela.*

Nyla: *¡Buen pensamiento! ¡Bueno es tiempo de irnos otra vez!*

If you want to go to a school like Michigan Tech, what school subjects should you study extra hard?

¿Si deseas ir a una Universidad como Michigan Tech, cuales son las materias escolares que debes estudiar mas fuerte?

MICHIGAN STATE UNIVERSITY

José: We are in East Lansing, Michigan.

Nyla: That's right!

Emjay: Michigan State University (MSU)!

Shay: Home of the Spartans and "Sparty" the Mascot.

Nyla: This campus is very big and there are over 45,000 students here.

José: MSU was known for animal and forest studies and is the only university with three medical schools on campus.

Shay: They also have good sports teams.

Emjay: Yep!

UNIVERSIDAD DE MICHIGAN STATE

José: *Estamos en el este de Lansing, Michigan.*

Nyla: *¡Así es!*

Emjay: *¡Universidad Estatal de Michigan (UEM)!*

Shay: *La casa de los Espartanos y de la mascota "Sparty."*

Nyla: *Este campus es muy grande y hay más de 45,000 estudiantes aquí.*

José: *UEM es conocido por sus estudios sobre animales y bosques y también es la única universidad que tiene tres escuelas de medicina en su campus.*

Shay: *También tienen buenos equipos de deportes.*

Emjay: *¡Sí!*

José: The football and basketball teams are really good!

Nyla: Ervin "Magic" Johnson played basketball here and TJ Duckett played football.

Little Brother: Wow! Magic Johnson and TJ Duckett!

Little Sister: My brother loves football and basketball. I only like football.

Emjay: Sports are a big part of some colleges. Some students gain athletic scholarships and get an education for free.

Shay: That's right; my brother had an athletic scholarship for college.

Little Sister: Free school sounds good to me!

Shay: Well before we go home, everyone say goodbye to Sparty the mascot.

How can students who play sports go to college for free?

Jose: ¡Los equipos de fútbol americano y de básquetbol son muy buenos!

Nyla: Ervin "Magic" Johnson jugo básketbol aquí and TJ Duckett jugo fútbol americano.

Hermano menor: ¡Wow! ¡Ervin "Magic" Johnson y TJ Duckett!

Hermana menor: A mi hermano le encanta el fútbol americano y el básquetbol. A mi nada más me gusta el fútbol americano.

Emjay: Los deportes son una gran parte de algunas universidades. Algunos estudiantes ganan becas atléticas y consiguen una educación gratis.

Shay: Así es; mi hermano tenía una beca deportiva para la universidad.

Hermana menor: ¡La escuela gratis me suena bien!

Shay: Bien, antes de irnos a casa, todos despídanse de la mascota Sparty.

¿Como pueden estudiantes que juegan deportes atender la universidad gratis?

36

YOU CAN GO TO COLLEGE

Nyla: Remember, you can make it to college!

José: Yeah, it is never too early to prepare for college!

Emjay: We know that many students deal with family problems, issues with friends, and many others. But please stay focused and prepare yourself for college.

Shay: I agree! Remember, we are always here but you can also talk to your school counselor. Call on us if you need us!

PUEDEN IR A LA UNIVERSIDAD

Nyla: Recuerden, si pueden llegar a la universidad.

José: Si, nunca es muy temprano para empezar a prepararse para la universidad.

Emjay: Sabemos que muchos estudiantes tienen problemas familiares, problemas con amigos, y muchos más. Pero, por favor manténganse enfocados y prepárense para la universidad.

Shay: ¡Yo estoy de acuedo! Recuerden siempre estaremos aquí, pero tambien pueden hablar con su consejero escolar. Llamenos si nos necesitan.

Little Brother: Bye!

Little Sister: Bye!

Hermano menor: ¡Adiós!

Hermana menor: ¡Adiós!

DEFINITIONS/GLOSSARY

College - a building used for educational purpose

College Application - forms that must be completed for the possibility of being accepted to a particular college

Financial Aid - money intended to help students pay educational related expenses including tuition, fees, room and board, books and other supplies for education

Scholarships - money or other aid granted to a student because of merit, need, etc., to pursue his or her studies

Grants - grant to a person or school for some educational project

Loans - designed to help students pay for college tuition, books, living expenses, etc. Loans are different from scholarships or grants because students need to pay this money back.

DEFINICIONES/GLOSARIO

Universidad – un edificio con un proposito educativo.

Aplicación para la Universidad- Formularios que son llenados con la posibiladad de ser aceptado a una Universidad.

Ayuda Financiera – Dinero dado con la intencion de ayudar a los estudiantes con gastos relacionados con la educacion incluyendo colegiatura, cobros, alojiamento y comida, libros and otros utiles escolares.

Becas- Dinero u otra ayuda dado a estudiantes basado en merito, necesidades, etc para lograr sus estudios superiores.

Subvención – Dado a una persona o escuela para un proyecto educativo.

Prestamos – Diseñados para ayudar a los estudiantes con la colegiatura, libros, gastos de vivienda. Prestamos son diferentes a las becas o subvenciónes porque los estudiantes necesitan pagar el prestamo.

Dorms - a building with rooms used for college students to live

SAT - a test used by some colleges during their admissions process

ACT - a test used by some colleges during their admissions process

Dormitorios – *Un edificio con habitaciones donde viven los universitarios.*

SAT – *un examen usado por las universidades durante el proceso de admisión.*

ACT – *un examen usado por las universidades durante el proceso de admisión.*

RESOURCES

Federal Student Aid:
www.fafsa.ed.gov

College Board
www.collegeboard.org

Future 4 Teens
www.future4teens.com

Number 2
www.number2.com

Joe Johnson
www.joejohnsonspeaks.com

RECURSOS

Ayuda Federal para Estudiantes:
www.fafsa.ed.gov

Junta de Directores
www.collegeboard.org

Futuro 4 Teens
www.future4teens.com

Número 2
www.number2.com

Joe Johnson
www.joejohnsonspeaks.com

THANK YOU

Future 4 Teens
The Kalamazoo Promise
Hispanic American Council
Western Michigan University
Michigan Technological University
Wayne State University
Michigan State University
University of Michigan
Dr. Maria Coady
Nancy Perez
Melisa Lopez
Stephanie Gómez

GRACIAS

Future 4 Teens
La Promesa de Kalamazoo
Consular Hispano-Americano
Western Michigan University
Michigan Technological University
Wayne State University
Michigan State University
University of Michigan
Dr. Maria Coady
Nancy Perez
Melisa Lopez
Stephanie Gómez

JOE JOHNSON|SPEAKS

Joe Johnson Biography

Joe Johnson was born in Milwaukee, WI but has lived in several places during his childhood including Hawaii and New York. He considers Milwaukee, AKA: "The Mil" his hometown because of the family ties.

Joe Johnson understands the meaning of struggle but has lived with a mentality instilled in him by his mother, "I can do and be anything I want in life." Johnson learned the value of education from both parents but as he began his love for sports at an early age, his focus with competing on the football field and basketball court caused him to develop a "who cares" attitude toward his education.

Growing up in the inner-city of Milwaukee allowed for Johnson to almost fall victim to what many young males were doing in his neighborhood. Sports were his key out of a city where many black and Latino males were often victims of gang violence and self-destruction. After becoming a high school standout football and basketball player, his education finally caught up with him when Division 1 colleges passed on him when finding out his grade point average

(1.6) and his score of 13 on the ACT (standardized test). After taking the long route by attending community college then enrolling in a university, he understood education and its affect but he continued his mediocre classroom habits with hopes of playing professional football. Although the opportunity to play professional football was close, his dream faded away and Johnson was stuck graduating with his 2.4 college grade point average and no plans about his future.

Johnson soon learned the power of competing in the classroom, the same way he competed in sports. With his new found attitude and focus, he began to excel academically after being accepted into a Master's program. Johnson began to love learning and realized his purpose was working with the youth and allowing others to be inspired by his voice.

As a proud graduate of Milwaukee Bay View high school, Johnson holds a Bachelor of Arts degree in Business from Saginaw Valley State University and a Master's degree in Counselor Education from Western Michigan University, Johnson is now in pursuit of a PhD. in Counselor Education at the University of Florida and ready to take on the world!

Made in the USA
Columbia, SC
22 February 2018

8969280R00029